POLAR BEARS

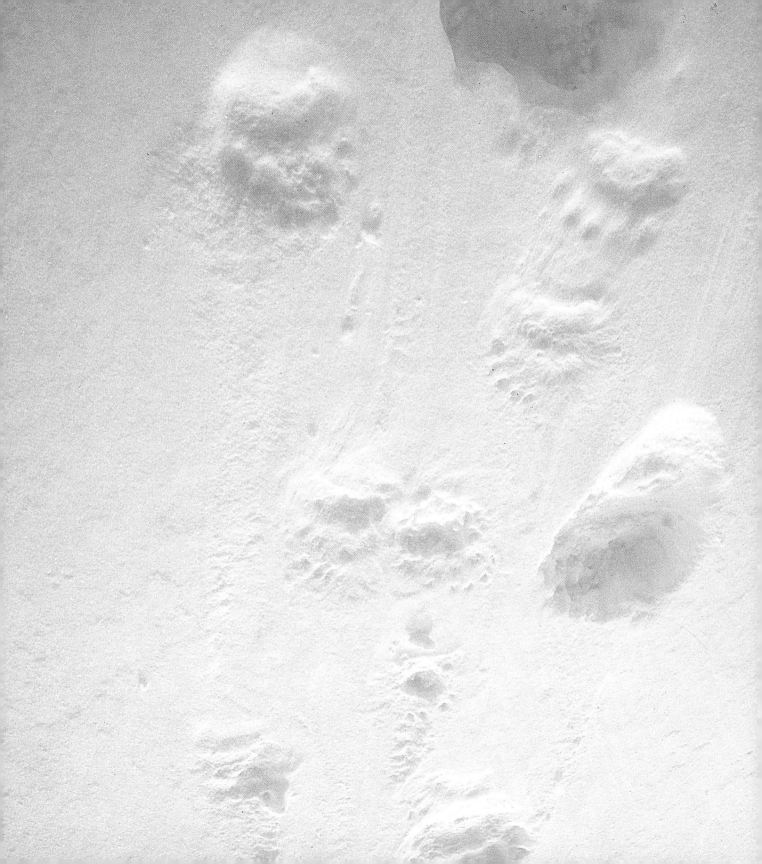

POLAR BEARS

A Carolrhoda Nature Watch Book

by Dorothy Hinshaw Patent
photographs by William Muñoz

Carolrhoda Books, Inc. / Minneapolis

For Frank Tyro and Barry Gordon

Text copyright © 2000 by Dorothy Hinshaw Patent
Photographs copyright © 2000 by William Muñoz

Additional photographs reproduced through the courtesy
of: WorldWild Nature and Stock Photography, © Beth
Davidow, pp. 12, 15; © B & C Alexander, pp. 19, 20, 21
(top), 23, 24, 25, 39, 40, 41; © Dorothy Patent, pp. 22, 27;
© Gary Schultz, p. 44.

Carolrhoda Books, Inc.
A Division of Lerner Publishing Group
241 First Avenue North
Minneapolis, MN 55401 U.S.A.

Website address: www.lernerbooks.com

LIBRARY OF CONGRESS CATALOGING-IN-PUBLICATION DATA

Patent, Dorothy Hinshaw.
    Polar Bears / by Dorothy Hinshaw Patent ; photographs
by William Muñoz.
        p. cm.
    "A Carolrhoda nature watch book."
    Summary: Describes the physical characteristics, diet,
natural habitat, and life cycle of polar bears.
    ISBN 1–57505–020–X (alk. paper)
    1. Polar bear—Juvenile literature. [1. Polar bear. 2.
Bears.] I. Muñoz, William, ill. II. Title.
QL737.C27P3627 2000
599.786—dc21   99-29601

Manufactured in the United States of America
1 2 3 4 5 6 – JR – 05 04 03 02 01 00

CONTENTS

KING OF THE ARCTIC

I look from the window of the warm bus near Churchill, Manitoba, in northern Canada, to see a polar bear asleep, lying right on the ice. The temperature is close to 0°F (–18°C), and a bitter wind is blowing. But the polar bear is napping comfortably, all wrapped up in its own fabulous fur coat. For the polar bear, this weather is mild—nothing compared to the Arctic winter, when –30°F (–34°C) is normal.

Wild polar bears are found only in the Arctic—one of the harshest areas in the world—and around Hudson Bay in northern Canada. The ground in the Arctic is permanently frozen, in some places for many feet. Trees cannot put down roots and grow. This treeless land is called the tundra. Only a few land animals thrive in the barren North, and the polar bear is the biggest and strongest of them all.

The polar bear is a relative newcomer on the planet. This giant creature evolved, or changed slowly over time, from the brown bear in the far North about 100,000 years ago. It still roams the Arctic, walking easily over ice and snow and swimming for miles through freezing cold water. Indeed, the polar bear is the "King of the Arctic."

Polar bears, like other bears, have short legs, stocky bodies, and short tails.

BEARS OF THE WORLD

The polar bear is one of eight **species,** or kinds, of bears. Bears are easy to recognize. They have short legs, stocky bodies, and short tails. Each foot has five toes. Bears walk the same way we do, on the flat of the foot. Their eyes face forward, and their ears are relatively small. Bears are large animals. Even the smallest, the Malayan sun bear, weighs up to 144 pounds (65 kg), as much as an adult person.

Along with animals like wolves, cats, and weasels, bears are members of a group called **carnivores,** or meat eaters. But unlike some other carnivores, most bears don't eat just meat. Bears such as the brown bear and the spectacled bear eat more plant foods like grass and fruit than they do meat. The panda rarely eats anything but bamboo.

Bears belong to the family scientists call the **Ursidae.** Most kinds of bears live in Asia, Europe, and North America. The brown bear lives on all three continents, but in most of western Europe, the brown bear is rare or extinct. In parts of North America, the brown bear is called the grizzly. The American black bear is found only in North America. It lives mostly in the woods and is rarely seen.

The American black bear is a relative of the polar bear. American black bears are found only in North America.

The sloth bear uses its lips to suck up termites.

Four kinds of bears live only in Asia. The Malayan sun bear has a short, dark coat, usually with a "necklace" of light fur. It uses its powerful front claws to rip open trees as it searches for bees' nests, termites, and insect larvae. It also rips apart and eats the growing tips of coconut palms. The Asiatic black bear lives throughout much of Asia, including Japan, but it favors hilly forests. The Indian sloth bear lives only in southern Asia. This shaggy, black bear specializes in eating termites, which it sucks up using its long muzzle, or snout, and flexible lips.

The giant panda is limited to bamboo forests in the mountains of China. Over time, the panda has developed a special extra "thumb," or spur, for holding onto bamboo shoots while it feeds. For many years, scientists weren't sure whether the panda was a kind of bear or a giant relative of the raccoon. But research shows that the panda is definitely a bear.

Only one type of bear lives in South America. The spectacled bear, named for the white circles that often ring its eyes, is a rare animal that feeds mostly on fruit. The spectacled bear is disappearing because its forest homes are being cut down rapidly.

The polar bear, which scientists call *Ursus maritimus,* is the largest of bears. Only an occasional male Kodiak, or coastal brown bear from Alaska, can match a big male polar bear in size. Female polar bears weigh 330 to 660 pounds (150–300 kg). Most males weigh about twice as much as females. A rare adult male polar bear can weigh close to a ton. When one of these giants rears up on its hind legs, it can stand 10 feet (3 m) tall!

Below: *The adult male polar bear* (left) *can weigh almost twice as much as the female* (right).
Opposite page: *Polar bears are completely comfortable in the cold north and think nothing of curling up for a nap in a snowbank.*

A trait shared by bears that live where winters are cold is their ability to **hibernate.** That means the bear's body goes into a resting state. The bear digs a den in the fall and stays there until springtime. A hibernating bear's heart and breathing slow down. The bear sleeps much of the time, but it can wake up if disturbed. It doesn't eat, drink, or emit wastes. When hibernating, the body burns only fat stored in its body for energy. As the fat is broken down, it provides the water the body needs as well as the energy.

Of the polar bears, only pregnant females always den up for the winter to give birth to their cubs and nurse them through the winter months. Sometimes, if the winter weather is especially bad, other polar bears will den up for a short time. It is more common, however, for polar bears to wander over the ice during the winter, hunting seals.

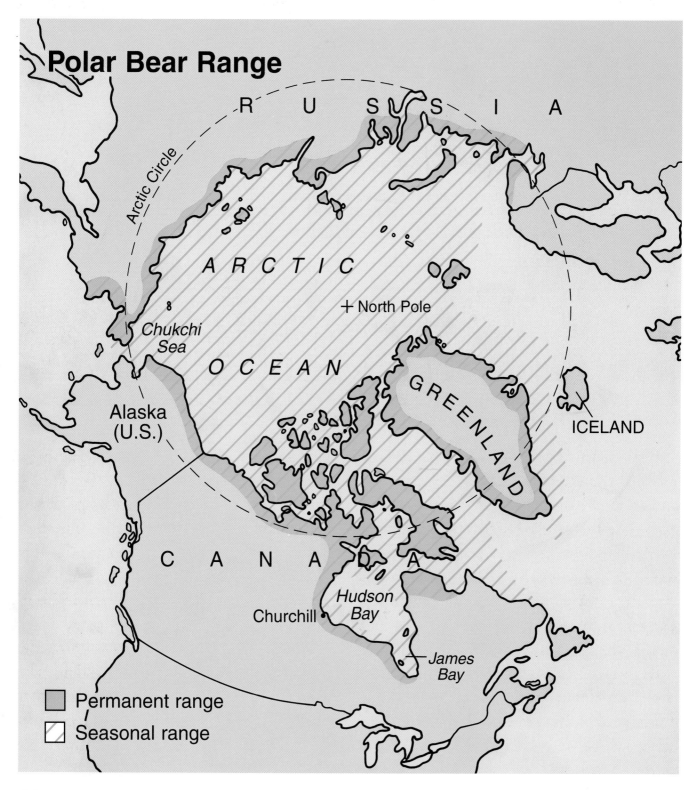

Polar Bear Range

R U S S I A

Arctic Circle

A R C T I C

+ North Pole

Chukchi
Sea

O C E A N

Alaska
(U.S.)

GREENLAND

ICELAND

C A N A D A

Churchill

Hudson
Bay

James
Bay

Permanent range

Seasonal range

14

In the Hudson Bay area, polar bears sometimes look for food along the shore and farther inland when the ice melts in the spring and summer months.

Little is known about polar bears over most of the Arctic. The region is so vast and so harsh that studying the bears isn't easy. The best-studied bears are those living in Arctic Canada and around Hudson Bay. The Hudson Bay bears live the farthest south of all the world's polar bears. They are the only polar bears that spend part of the year away from ice and snow.

During the spring and summer when the ice melts, polar bears living in Hudson Bay are forced to look for food along the shore and farther inland. The polar bears eat little or nothing. As it gets warmer, they travel inland and dig a den. They dig down to the layer of permanent ice under the ground, called the **permafrost.** Here, they may live in dens when they're unable to find food. Unlike other bear species, if a polar bear hasn't eaten in 10 to 14 days, its body may switch to the body chemistry of hibernation for a short time—even in the summertime. The ability to change the body's chemistry in this way helps polar bears survive in a region where food may be unavailable for months at a time.

In the fall, the male bears and females who are not pregnant travel back to the shore. Many of them gather near the town of Churchill, Manitoba, on the bay's southwest shore, where they wait for the ice to form. This concentration of polar bears is unique and brings scientists and travelers from around the world to study and observe.

Polar bears generally live solitary lives, but in Churchill, Manitoba, observers sometimes catch sight of a group of polar bears.

Polar bears have thick fur that helps protect them from the harsh Arctic climate.

PHYSICAL CHARACTERISTICS

Polar bears are suited for their life in the cold, icy North in many ways. The polar bear has a thick coat of fur, with soft, dense underfur and long, coarse **guard hairs.** The guard hairs are hollow, which helps insulate, or protect, the bear from the cold. The polar bear's coat looks white because the air spaces in each hair scatter light of all colors. Under the skin is a layer of fat, called **blubber,** almost 5 inches (13 cm) thick, which helps insulate the body.

Polar bears use their huge paws like snowshoes on land.

Polar bears are amazingly strong animals, yet they are also quick. They can run at a speed of 30 to 35 miles per hour (48–56 km) for short distances. A polar bear's huge paws, which may be a foot (30.5 cm) wide, serve as snowshoes on land. Thick fur on the bottoms of a polar bear's feet help keep it from slipping on the snow and ice. Sharp claws help both in gripping the ice and piercing the thick skin of seals.

Polar bears are fine swimmers. When a polar bear swims, it holds its hind feet together and uses them to steer. The front paws, which have partial webbing between the toes, make powerful paddles. The head and shoulders of a polar bear form a wedge shape that helps it pass smoothly through the water. Its long neck allows it to stretch its head up above the water while swimming. A polar bear can swim for 20 miles (32 km) through the frigid Arctic water without getting too cold.

Polar bears are strong swimmers.

A polar bear has keen senses. Both its hearing and its eyesight are good. A polar bear must be able to see well in the dark, for the sun does not rise for weeks on end during winter in the far North. But its eyes also must withstand the glare of the sun across white snow. Most sensitive of all is the bear's sense of smell. It can smell a seal under 3 feet (0.9 m) of snow from 0.6 mile (1 km) away.

Polar bears have excellent eyesight.

Polar bears usually eat meat. This one is eating a duck (left). Polar bears sometimes eat plants or algae. This polar bear is eating kelp, a kind of algae (below).

HUNTING FOR FOOD

Of all bears, the polar bear eats the most meat. Its favorite prey is seals, especially ringed seals, which it hunts across the Northern ice that covers the seawater. Polar bears will also feast on the carcasses of dead whales or walruses that wash ashore. At the southern edge of the Arctic, they eat geese, grasses, and fall berries, or forage for mussels and seaweed along the shore before the ice forms.

Understanding the ice is important to understanding how polar bears hunt. When ice forms over the sea, it doesn't make an even layer like a skating rink. At first, the ice is thin enough for the wind and waves to break it into pieces. When water coats the broken, jagged edges, they become rounded. These round, flat pieces are called **pan ice.** Very large pans, which can extend for miles, are called **ice floes.** As the pieces of ice get colder, they get thicker. They join together to make larger blocks. Eventually, as the thermometer plunges into deep winter, the blocks freeze together, forming **pack ice.**

Pack ice is large blocks of pan ice frozen together.

Two Inuit hunters look for polar bears while sitting on top of pressure ridges.

Some of the pack ice doesn't stay still. It slowly moves in a clockwise direction around the North Pole. The ice that circulates around the pole is called the **polar pack.** Ice that stays bound to the shore or to the sea bottom is called **fast ice.** Between the polar pack and the fast ice is the **shear zone,** where blocks of ice are jammed together and torn apart. When the giant floes of ice push up against one another, the ice in the contact area becomes jumbled together into piles of blocks called **pressure ridges.** Pressure ridges can be 40-foot-tall (12.4 m) barriers made up of 10-foot (3m) chunks of ice thrown together and may extend for miles. For Arctic explorers, crossing pressure ridges with sleds carrying hundreds of pounds of supplies can be a nightmare. But polar bears lumber easily across them.

When the water or wind pulls blocks of ice apart, open stretches of water, called **leads,** form. During the frigid winter, leads are soon covered over with a layer of ice. But a seal will keep a hole open in the thin ice so it can surface for air. And where seals come up to breathe, polar bears hunt.

A ringed seal

A ringed seal has a number of breathing holes and uses each one often. The ice that covers the lead gradually gets thicker and thicker. As it thickens, the seal scrapes away any new ice with the claws on its flippers and rotates its body like a drill as it surfaces to keep the breathing hole open. In this way, the seal can still reach the surface to get vital air even when the leads disappear.

As time goes on, snow falls over the ice. The warm breath of the seal melts the snow closest to the water, hollowing out an area above the breathing hole. This area, roofed with ice and snow, is called an **aglu.**

When a polar bear finds a ringed seal's breathing hole, it may stay there, motionless, for hours, waiting for the seal to arrive. When the seal surfaces, the bear plunges through the ice, strikes the seal with a powerful front paw, grabs the seal with its teeth, and pulls the seal's body out onto the ice. A polar bear can kill a 200-pound (91 kg) ringed seal with just one strike of the paw and pull its 12-inch-thick (30 cm) body through a breathing hole that may be only a few inches in diameter. In the process, most of the bones in the seal's body may be broken.

A polar bear feasts on a ringed seal.

Polar bears are big, powerful hunters.

During the summer, polar bears may stalk seals that have come out onto the ice to bask in the sun. Polar bears will also swim underwater towards an ice floe, hoping to surprise a resting seal.

The easiest way for a polar bear to get a meal, however, is to hunt for seal pups. In the springtime, a female ringed seal gives birth to a single pup in a large aglu. At first, the pup isn't prepared for life in the water. While the mother seal hunts for food in the sea, she leaves her pup on the ice next to her breathing hole in the aglu. There, the pup can rest and wait for its mother's return. When a polar bear locates a pup by its scent, it breaks through the top of the aglu, and grabs the pup. If the mother is there, the bear grabs her too before she has a chance to escape into the water.

Like a polar bear, a seal has a thick layer of blubber under its skin. Normally, a bear eats only the skin and blubber of its prey. This may seem strange, since a seal's body has a lot of meat, or muscle. But digesting the meat requires a great deal of water. The only freshwater available to a polar bear is in the form of ice or snow. Eating enough ice or snow to digest the meat would cool the bear's body too much. Digesting the fat in the blubber, however, releases both energy and water that the bear's body can use. The skin provides vitamins that the bear needs.

Because conditions allow polar bears to hunt only part of the year, they must work hard to find enough food to carry them through the lean months. When food is available, at least half their time is spent hunting. About 2 percent of their attempts at catching seals are successful. Even when prey is most abundant, an experienced adult bear lands a seal only every 4 to 5 days. But when it feeds, it feasts. A polar bear can eat as much as 150 pounds (68 kg) of blubber at one meal.

Two polar bears at Churchill, waiting for the ice to freeze solid.

Two young male polar bears play-fight. The skills they practice here will help them when they are old enough to fight over females.

FAMILY LIFE

Polar bears are basically solitary animals. Males only interact with other bears during the mating season or when they find themselves in the same place at the same time, such as at Churchill before the bay freezes over. If a male comes across another male, the males may fight to see who is strongest. They may break teeth and suffer wounds during their battles.

Polar bears mate between March and May. Scientists think the males locate the females by scent. When a male finds a possible mate, the bears approach one another, bobbing their heads. Once they have paired up, the male stays with the female for several days. During that time, he keeps her away from other males. The pair may hunt and rest together. After mating, they go their separate ways. Both the male and the female may mate with several other polar bears during the mating season.

A mother polar bear rests with her two young cubs.

In the fall, pregnant female polar bears dig dens in the snow and hibernate. Most of them den on land or on the fast ice. But in some areas, such as the Beaufort Sea, about half the bears den on the pack ice. From the time a female bear enters her den until she and her cubs come out, the ice may have drifted hundreds of miles. Scientists don't know how the bears can orient themselves and find food in an unfamiliar place.

Raising the young is left completely to the mother. The young, usually two cubs, are born between late November and early January, from 6.5 to 9 months after mating. Newborn polar bear cubs weigh less than 2 pounds (0.9 kg). They have little fur, their eyes are closed, and they cannot hear. But they do know how to find their mother's supply of rich milk. Polar bear milk is about 30 percent fat—only seals and whales have richer milk.

These cubs are nursing.

The cubs develop quickly. By the time they are 26 days old, they can hear, and by the time they are 33 days old, their eyes open. At 2 months old, they are furry balls of curiosity, wandering around the den and playing together.

The female bear eats nothing while in the den, so she may go 6 to 8 months without food or water. So during the months that she is hunting, she must put on about 400 pounds (182 kg) of fat to nourish herself and her cubs. That's as much as two large men weigh! The mother bear is quiet in the den and seems half asleep. But if she suspects a threat to her youngsters, such as an adult male bear or a human hunter, the mother can be wide awake in moments.

The bears usually leave the den in March or April, when the ringed seals give birth to their pups and hunting is easy. By this time, the cubs weigh about 22 to 33 pounds (10–15 kg) each. The family stays near the den for a week or more while the cubs get used to life in the outside world. Then the mother takes the cubs out on the pack ice, where they begin the long process of learning to hunt by watching her.

As the cubs grow older, they start to learn about life from their mother (above). *They also take time for a rest in the snow* (inset).

These cubs are almost full grown. Soon, they'll leave their mother and be on their own.

The cubs usually stay with their mother until they are at least 2 years old. By then, they have learned how and where to catch their own food and dig a den. A polar bear is ready to mate when it is 5 or 6 years old and weighs 330 to 660 pounds (150–300 kg). By this time, a female may be full grown. Male polar bears continue to grow and may not reach their full size until they are 10 or 11 years old. Wild polar bears have been known to live 30 years. In a zoo, however, they can live even longer.

Churchill, Manitoba

POLAR BEARS AND PEOPLE

The polar bears of Churchill, Manitoba, can cause trouble. An adult male polar bear has no predators other than humans and is basically fearless of people unless he has been hunted. Polar bears don't generally attack people—the bears tend to ignore anything that is not a seal. But they are so powerful that just one swat from a bear's paw can break a person's neck. In the past, people have been killed or seriously injured by bears around Churchill. The town garbage dump used to be open, and bears would go there to rummage for food. The people of Churchill have fenced off the dump, but some bears still head in that direction. Bear traps are set on the routes leading to town and the dump to capture wayward bears. Once a bear is trapped, it is put in "bear jail" until the ice forms. Then it is released.

Near Churchill, bears that get too close to town may be trapped (left). *Trapped bears are put in the polar bear jail* (above).

The town is right on the path the bears take to go to Cape Churchill, east of the town, in search of the ice in October and November. Most of the bears pass by the town or travel through unseen at night. But sometimes, people encounter a bear on the streets of the town. The government has developed the Polar Bear Alert program to educate the people of Churchill and to help avoid trouble with bears. Polar Bear Alert gives talks to schools and community organizations on how to be careful during the bear season. Don't walk around a corner if you can't see what's on the other side, they are told, and don't walk around town at night. If you see a bear in town, stay away from it and call Polar Bear Alert right away. The program gets hundreds of calls each season. If a bear is seen in town, officials do their best to chase it out or capture it. Captured bears are taken to the bear jail. Altogether, at least two to three dozen bears end up in the jail each year.

Tundra buggies take tourists and scientists to observe polar bears.

Most of the Churchill bears stay away from town. They aren't interested in people. They are waiting for the ice to form so they can hunt seals again. The ice first forms off the shore of Cape Churchill. There, the bears gather to wait. And there, tourists and scientists gather to watch the bears. The most common way to see the bears is by **tundra buggy.** A tundra buggy is a bus fitted with gigantic tires that can roll across the tundra without getting bogged down, even when the ground is partially thawed. From the safety of the tundra buggy, people watch the bears. Mostly, the bears sleep, snuggled into the snow or sprawled out on the ice. The people shiver in the bitter wind, but the bears are completely comfortable. Often, a couple of young male bears will come together and play-fight. They rear up on their hind legs and swat at each other, then wrestle like professionals. In photographs, these encounters look like fights. But the bears move slowly and are careful to be gentle with one another.

Some people object to the tundra buggies. A hot lunch is served on the buggies, and the smell of the food attracts the bears. The hungry bears come right up to the buggies and even rear up on their back paws trying to get at the food. Some scientists and others worry that bears that get used to the buggies will lose any fear they have of humans and will come to associate people with food.

A polar bear investigates a tundra buggy up close.

An Inuit hunter carries a long spear, which he'll use to hunt polar bears.

POLAR BEAR DANGERS

In countries with polar bears, governments regulate bear hunting. But native Northern peoples have always hunted polar bears and valued their hides and meat. In addition, native people of the Arctic consider killing a polar bear to be a brave act of manhood that brings respect. Until rifles were invented, hunting polar bears required great courage. The only way to kill a bear was to get close to it. The hunter used a 5-to-6-foot-long (1.5–1.8 m) spear. The spear had a sharp tip made from jade, ivory, or copper.

An Inuit hunter and his dogs hunt polar bears.

When an Inuit man (Inuit women were rarely, if ever, hunters) was out on the ice with his sled and team of dogs, he would eagerly follow any fresh polar bear tracks. When he caught up to the bear, he would let his dogs loose. The dogs would dash forward and surround the bear, snapping at it from all sides. The attack by the dogs would confuse and tire the bear, and the hunter would finally step in and spear it.

If more than one man was involved in the hunt, the man who first spotted the bear got the pelt. Polar bear fur makes beautiful, warm pants. It also makes good covers for boots that muffle the sound of a hunter's feet. A hunter might also use the hide to make a white shield to hide him as he sneaked up on seals.

An Inuit sews polar bear fur into pants.

The rest of the bear was divided up among the hunters. Some Inuit like to eat polar bear meat. Polar bear bones are strong and can be fashioned into a variety of tools.

In addition to the native people of the Arctic hunting polar bears, trophy hunters—people who want hides to display—also come north to hunt bears. Trophy hunting became popular after rifles became common.

Until the mid-1970s, the numbers of polar bears in the world were decreasing, largely due to the combination of native and trophy hunting. Polar bears live on the territory of five countries, including Canada, the United States, and Russia. They also live around Greenland, a territory of Denmark, and the Svalbard Islands, which belong to Norway. The five polar bear nations got together to plan ways of helping the bears. Under the International Union for the Conservation of Nature (IUCN) Polar Bear Agreement, most hunting of polar bears was banned, and scientific studies were designed.

In the United States, polar bears are also protected by the Marine Mammal Protection Act, which allows hunting only by Alaskan natives. In Canada, no hunting is allowed in some provinces, such as Manitoba. In others, such as the Northwest Territories, each village receives a set number of hunting permits each year. The villages keep some of the permits for their young hunters and sell a few to trophy hunters for about $10,000 each.

The five polar bear nations have come together to save the polar bear.

In areas where polar bears can be studied, populations are steady or are increasing.

The Arctic is such a difficult environment to explore that scientists don't know how many polar bears are alive. Estimates run between 20,000 and 40,000. The protection given to bears by the agreements among the polar bear nations seems to be working. In areas where the bears can be studied, the populations remain steady or are increasing. But many threats to polar bears still exist.

Many polar bears live on the ice of the Chukchi Sea, a part of the Arctic Ocean between Alaska and Russia. Most of these bears den in Russia. Scientists fear that unregulated hunting there is killing too many bears. In addition, recent oil spills in Siberia (a part of Russia) have flowed down rivers into the Arctic Ocean and may harm the bears or their prey.

The Arctic National Wildlife Refuge contains oil reserves that might one day be tapped.

Oil drilling can also be a threat to Arctic animals in both Russia and Alaska. Wrangel Island, which belongs to Russia, and the area of the Alaskan coast that is protected as the Arctic National Wildlife Refuge contain oil reserves that might be tapped in the future. Oil spills in either area would be a disaster to all Arctic wildlife, including polar bears. About 45 percent of Alaska's pregnant polar bears den on or near the Arctic National Wildlife Refuge, and scientists fear they could be driven away by the disturbances accompanying drilling.

In parts of the Arctic, such as some Norwegian islands, dangerous chemicals from pollution are accumulating in the bodies of polar bears. No one can be sure what effects these may have on the polar bears' ability to survive and reproduce.

Perhaps the worst threat to the bears and other animals adapted to life in the icy North is global warming. The average temperature on Earth rose almost one degree Fahrenheit (0.5°C) over the last 100 years. If our planet continues to warm up, the longer ice-free period would mean a shorter hunting season for the bears, since they depend on the Arctic ice for hunting. As it is, polar bears in some areas must eat enough in only 3 or 4 months to last through the rest of the year.

Whatever threatens polar bears probably threatens all life in the Arctic. We can hope that the international efforts to study and save the polar bear and its home will succeed, ensuring that this magnificent creature remains King of the Arctic.

Scientists continue their efforts to study and protect the polar bear.

GLOSSARY

aglu: domed space formed above a seal's breathing hole as snow accumulates over the ice

blubber: a thick layer of fat, located under the skin

carnivores: meat eaters, such as bears

evolve: to change slowly over time

fast ice: ice that stays bound to the shore or to the sea bottom

guard hairs: hollow hairs that help insulate polar bears from the cold

hibernate: to stay in a resting state throughout the winter

ice floes: very large floating pieces of ice

leads: open stretches of water formed by the forces of rotation of the polar pack, or by the wind pulling blocks of ice apart

pack ice: blocks of ice frozen together

pan ice: floating pieces of ice with rounded edges

permafrost: a layer of earth that is permanently frozen under the ground

polar pack: ice that circulates around the pole

pressure ridges: piles of ice blocks formed from giant chunks of ice that bumped against one another

shear zone: area between the polar pack and the fast ice, where blocks of ice slide past one another

species: kinds

tundra: treeless land in the Arctic region

tundra buggy: a bus fitted with gigantic tires that can roll across the tundra without getting bogged down, even when the ground is partially thawed

Ursidae: family to which bears belong

INDEX

ABOUT THE AUTHOR

Dorothy Hinshaw Patent was born in Minnesota and spent most of her growing-up years in Marin County, California. She has a Ph.D. in zoology from the University of California. Dr. Patent is the author of over 100 nonfiction books for children, including *Apple Trees* and *Wild Turkeys*, published by Lerner Publications, and *Baby Horses, Dogs: The Wolf Within, Horses,* and *Cattle,* published by Carolrhoda Books, Inc. She has also co-authored gardening books and a cookbook for adults. She has two grown sons and lives in Missoula, Montana, with her husband, Greg.

ABOUT THE PHOTOGRAPHER

William Muñoz traveled to Churchill, Manitoba, to photograph polar bears for this book. He has worked as a nature photographer for over 20 years. You can see his pictures of animals and plants in many books for children. Some of these books are *Watchful Wolves, Ants, Apple Trees, Wild Turkeys,* and *Waiting Alligators,* published by Lerner Publications, and *Horses, Dogs: The Wolf Within,* and *Cattle,* published by Carolrhoda Books, Inc. William lives with his wife and son in western Montana.